What Participants Are Saying

WILD has been my graduate-level prepar~~ation for life and godliness. After~~ 14 years at home, it launched me into the marketplace and deposited me in a position where my strengths are used daily, my passions are well-satisfied, and God's purposes are being fulfilled in and through me. I'm living in my sweet spot because of WILD.

Sheila Shupp

WILD has been an incredible learning journey for me. It is a safe place to hone and grow your skills and confidence. I am so thankful that I was included in this community of strong, encouraging, and zesty women who all have unique expressions of the same heart: we love Jesus.

Lauren Dunn

WILD is a journey to unlock the gifting and calling God has for your life. I can pinpoint the time in my life when my eyes were opened to see myself as God sees me. The process began when I said *yes* to WILD, and I am so thankful that I did.

Lisa Corley

WILD is wonderful—new friends, great teachings, challenging assignments, and the personal growth that comes from all these experiences. But what made the greatest impact on me is what Pastor Lynda Grove said at the first WILD class I attended. She asked, "What is our motivation for leadership?" It was a reminder and a challenge to each of us that what we do, on or off a platform, is not for our own gain. Everything we do is for God's glory.

Judy Brisky

I love how WILD created a forever sisterhood! The Lord made it clear that the WILD journey had only just begun.

Lucy Wallace

WOMEN IN LEADERSHIP DEVELOPMENT

Participant Journal

WiLD

WOMEN IN LEADERSHIP DEVELOPMENT

FROM GATEWAY WOMEN
FOREWORD BY DEBBIE MORRIS

Participant Journal

WILD Women in Leadership Development: Participant Journal
Copyright © 2018 by Gateway Women

ISBN: 978-1-945529-46-7 Paperback

We hope you hear from the Holy Spirit and receive God's richest blessings from this book by Gateway Press. We want to provide the highest quality resources that take the messages, music, and media of Gateway Church to the world. For more information on other resources from Gateway Publishing, go to gatewaypublishing.com.

Gateway Press, an imprint of Gateway Publishing
700 Blessed Way
Southlake, Texas 76092
gatewaypublishing.com

18 19 20 21 22   5 4 3 2 1
Printed in the United States of America

This book is dedicated to the women of Gateway Church.
You are beautiful leaders.
Thank you for the privilege of watching you grow in your gifts.
You make us all better, stronger, and more effective.

Table of Contents

Foreword

When we first pioneered Gateway Church, the Lord called me to Women's Ministry. I rose to the challenge, reluctantly at first, feeling more drafted than invited. But as I learned to lean into my position and not resist it, I found abundant grace and soon realized the calling suited me.

My heart became burdened for the preparation of the next generation of women as leaders and influencers. By this time, our women's ministry was well underway, yet I sensed there was more we could do to invest in Gateway Church's women. While hosting a leadership roundtable, the concept of a special development class for women leaders was proposed. Debbie Stuart, former Director of Women's Ministry at Prestonwood Baptist Church, shared her leadership development concept called WILD.

I was with Lynda Grove at the time, and we loved what we heard. We were eager to construct a curriculum that instilled leadership principles into the women of Gateway Church. We knew we needed to prepare women intentionally as leaders, and we desired to accomplish this through relationship. Debbie Stuart graciously gave us permission to use the WILD title, and we spent the next several months crafting the curriculum for our own WILD ministry. We launched that first class with expectant hearts.

Since then, the women's leadership team has been on an exciting journey. Through the relational training of WILD, we dedicate ourselves to helping Gateway Church's women rise to their fullest potential. We intentionally keep WILD classes small to create an atmosphere that allows enduring bonds of friendship between the staff and our women, as well as among the women themselves.

Although completing the class does not guarantee a leadership position, it has propelled many women into the next stage of their destinies. Some have started ministries, businesses, and magazines. Others have written books and taken leadership roles with great purpose and confidence, both inside and outside the church. The testimonies from the women of WILD are so inspiring. I love what Lauren Dunn says of her time in WILD: "It provides a safe place to step into your own skin." And Sheila Shupp says, "WILD is my kind of fun! It's like positioning yourself under a great mother's purposeful training. In WILD, I finally grasped how perfectly I am made. I learned how my strengths work together and how to use them for kingdom purposes."

WILD provides a great opportunity for you to develop your gifts and receive the training you need to be equipped for excellence in leadership. I am excited for you as you embark on your journey. I pray you, too, will find abundant grace and fulfillment as you realize your calling and step into all God has for you.

Debbie Morris
Executive Pastor, Gateway Women
Gateway Church

Acknowledgments

We are better together!

From its strategy to its content, from the initial dream to the present reality, WILD was developed in an atmosphere of relationship and designed to be implemented the same way. Because of such focus on relationship, many people were involved in the birth and development of this training.

Thank you, Pastor Mallory Bassham, Dr. Cassie Reid, and the Gateway Women's leadership team, for your contributions to the development of the content and teaching of WILD. You have helped shape the heart and message of this ministry. Many graduates have been forever impacted by your love and service.

Thank you, Dana Stone, for compiling the first Leader Guide and for bravely taking a variety of teachings, activations, and ideas and turning them into something wonderful. You took vision and brought it to life. There wouldn't be anything to share with others without you and your gifts.

Thank you, Jen de LaPorte and Christy Linder, for helping us develop the Participant Journal and for assisting us in taking this manuscript across the finish line.

Thank you, Pastor Phillip Hunter, for developing the Bible study technique, the *Promise Principle™*, and thank you, Gateway Church, for allowing us to use excerpts from *The Promise Principle Journal*.

Over the years several key lay leaders have served the women of Gateway Church through WILD. Thank you, Penny Spurling, Lisa Corley, and Mari Eisenrich, for your selfless devotion to the gifts and callings of others. You've all been role models of godly leadership.

Of course, WILD wouldn't even exist without the vision and oversight of Pastor Debbie Morris. Pastor Debbie was the first to say that we have to find a way to identify and develop more women leaders. She's always been the champion of others, and WILD has been a way for her to make her personal passion come to life. Thank you, Pastor Debbie, for leading the way for all of us.

Thank you, Gateway Publishing, for taking these valuable teachings and shaping them into a curriculum for churches around the world. Craig Dunnagan, John Andersen, Kathy Krenzien, James Reid, Jenny Morgan, Peyton Sepeda, and Caleb Jobe all worked to make this a successful project.

Finally, we want to express our personal appreciation to the women of Gateway Church who have graciously allowed us to field test this material for years. Your beautiful faces and your amazing gifts have inspired us. You are treasures to the body of Christ, and we are so proud of you for honoring God with every ounce of your passion and leadership calling.

Hello Beautiful Friend

Welcome to WILD! We are excited about the journey you have just begun!

WILD (Women in Leadership Development) came from our desire to identify, develop, and encourage women leaders in our church more effectively. We wanted to entrust greater leadership and authority to these women, but we lacked both the personal relationship and the opportunity to invest our vision and values into their hearts. These needs led us to develop a plan of action to invest in emerging leaders like you.

God is WILD about you. He invites each one of us to an exciting adventure. We believe WILD is a life-changing experience. Not only will you make new friends, but you will also experience many insightful moments of self-discovery. Through a simple format of teaching, hearing God, and activation exercises, the Holy Spirit will move in your heart in miraculous ways. You will find this leadership journey is not about a particular position but rather about pressing into God to know yourself more thoroughly and to agree with Him about what makes you unique and special.

Perhaps you already serve in a variety of leadership roles, whether inside or outside the local church. Or maybe you are just embarking on your leadership journey, and you aren't sure what the future holds. Either way, let us reassure you. The many women who have already participated in this program have found themselves with a greater sense of belonging and purpose that propelled them further into their destinies.

This journal is designed to maximize your experience. Everything you need to participate fully in WILD is included here. In each session, you will find:

- a Character Builder to encourage the development of your godly character,
- space to take notes on the content of that session's teachings,
- information related to homework or special assignments,
- and space to record your thoughts and revelations from the class activations.

We hope this journal will become a priceless treasure and a remembrance of all that God did to develop and release you as a leader in His Kingdom.

We love you, and we are so excited to share this journey with you.

Lynda Grove
Pastor of Women
Gateway Church

WELCOME TO

WiLD

session

1

TO EVERYTHING THERE IS A SEASON,
and a time for every matter or purpose under heaven...
HE HAS MADE EVERYTHING BEAUTIFUL IN ITS TIME.
He also has planted eternity IN MEN'S HEARTS AND MINDS
(A DIVINELY IMPLANTED SENSE OF A PURPOSE
working through the ages which nothing under the sun but
GOD ALONE CAN SATISFY),
yet so that men cannot find out what GOD HAS DONE
FROM THE BEGINNING *to the* END...
I KNOW THAT WHATEVER GOD DOES,
IT ENDURES FOREVER;
nothing can be added to it NOR ANYTHING TAKEN FROM IT.
And God does it so that men will (reverently) fear Him (revere and worship Him,
KNOWING THAT HE IS).
ECCLESIASTES 3:1, 11, 14 (AMPC)

Character Builder

HUMILITY

Definition

- Being free from pride or arrogance
- Thinking of others above yourself (Romans 12:3; Proverbs 3:34)

Reading

Acts 11–15

Biblical Application

Barnabas was sent by the Jerusalem church to see what was happening in the church at Antioch. Then he went to Tarsus to seek Saul (later Paul). Barnabas paved the way for Paul's ministry. We see him first seeking Paul (Acts 11:25), then ministering alongside him (Acts 12–15) until they go their separate ways (Acts 15:38–39). Barnabas was not intimidated when asked to help someone else rise in leadership; he was happy to play his unique role.

Personal Application

- How often do you find yourself falsely discrediting your strengths, gifts, or accomplishments to gain more recognition?
- How do you respond when you receive compliments that acknowledge your gifts or a job you have done well?
- How do you respond when the credit or reward you deserve is overlooked or given to another person?

Teaching 1: The Vision and Purpose of WILD

1. Why Are You Here?

2. What Is the Vision of WILD?

3. What Is the Purpose of WILD?

4. What Can I Expect?

Activation: Getting to Know One Another

· • · • ● · • · •

This is the first of several activations you will experience in WILD.
Do your best to be transparent and have an open mind and heart.

· • · • ● · • · •

Take two minutes to think about and write down your answers to the following questions. Then be prepared to share your answers with the class.

1. What brought me here?

_____

_____

_____

_____

2. What do I expect to gain from this class?

_____

_____

_____

_____

_____

Teaching 2: Overview of WILD

All in the Mindset

Participant Journal

_____
_____

_____

Character Builder

_____
_____

_____

_____

Homework

_____
_____

_____

_____

Personal Reflection

_____
_____

_____

_____

The _Promise Principle_™

_____
_____

_____

(The following excerpts are taken from *The Promise Principle Journal*.)

Study Technique

The *Promise Principle* is based on 2 Peter 1:3–11. God has given us His promises to participate in His nature rather than live in our own nature. Our nature is to be ruled by our circumstances.

> In view of all this, make every effort to respond to God's promises (2 Peter 1:5 NLT).

How can I identify God's promises?

His promises are either a truth or a commandment.

How do I respond to God's promises?

1. Ask by faith (Matthew 21:22; James 4:2b)
2. Receive with thanks (1 Timothy 4:4; Ephesians 5:20)

Every truth and commandment is a promise from God. As you read, underline every promise from God and ask yourself if this is a promise you should ask God for in faith or receive with a thankful heart. Then pray it!

> Pray about everything (Philippians 4:6 NLT).

Example #1 from Ephesians

God decided in advance to adopt us into his own family by bringing us to himself through Jesus Christ. This is what he wanted to do, and it gave him great pleasure (Ephesians 1:5 NLT).

Is this a promise you should ask for in faith or receive with thanks?
Receive with thanks!
Ask the Holy Spirit how you need to respond to this promise based on the circumstances in your life. Then pray it.

Lord, there are times when I feel unloved and struggle with loneliness, but I thank You that You picked me and made me a part of Your family. I am loved by You. I belong! Thank You that You desire me, Amen.

Example #2 from Ephesians

Asking God, the glorious Father of our Lord Jesus Christ, to give you spiritual wisdom and insight so that you might grow in your knowledge of God. I pray that your hearts will be flooded with light so that you can understand the confident hope he has given to those he called—his holy people who are his rich and glorious inheritance (Ephesians 1:17–18 NLT).

Is this a promise you should ask for in faith or receive with thanks?
Ask for by faith!
Ask the Holy Spirit how you need to respond to this promise based on the circumstances in your life. Then pray it.

Lord, I want to know You and all that You have for me. I ask You to give me spiritual wisdom and insight. My desire is to grow in my knowledge of You. I need to know You because I feel despair, I am anxious, and I am filled with fear. Would You fill my heart with light and overcome the darkness? Help me to understand the hope that I have in You. I want You to be my confidence, Amen.

Recap

1. Underline the promises as you read.
2. Identify the promise as a truth or a commandment.
3. Ask the Holy Spirit what circumstance in your life is touched by this promise.
4. Do you need to ask, do you need to receive it, or both?
5. Pray it!
6. Journal what the Holy Spirit is saying to you.

GRACE AND PEACE BE MULTIPLIED TO YOU
in the knowledge of God and of JESUS OUR LORD;
SEEING THAT HIS DIVINE POWER has granted to us everything
PERTAINING TO LIFE AND GODLINESS,
THROUGH THE TRUE KNOWLEDGE OF HIM
Who called us by His own glory and excellence.
FOR BY THESE HE HAS GRANTED TO US
His precious and magnificent promises,
SO THAT BY THEM YOU MAY BECOME PARTAKERS
of the DIVINE NATURE
2 PETER 1:2-4 (NASB)

Homework: Practice Personal Reflection

· • · • ● · • • ·

The homework for Session 1 is to practice Personal Reflection.
Personal Reflection is a great tool to help you grow in an ongoing pattern
of dialogue with God about matters of your heart.
Beginning in Session 2, you will receive homework assignments to be completed
and shared in the next session. These will consist of activities and questions
designed to help you process what God is saying to you and assist in your
understanding of the material being presented in class.

· • · ● • · • ·

These thought-provoking questions are designed to be used during your personal quiet times to prepare your heart for the upcoming session.

1. **What are you asking God for in this class? Make a list of your responses.**

_____

_____

_____

_____

_____

_____

_____

_____

2. In what area(s) of your life would you like to see growth in leadership?

3. Where would you like to serve?

The *Promise Principle*

· • · • ● · • · • ·

Each session includes an opportunity for you to read Scripture and use the Promise Principle. After using this technique, there are two additional questions designed to help you grow in your understanding of God's character.

· • · • ● · • · • ·

Read Ephesians 1

1. Underline the promises as you read.
2. Identify the promise as a truth or a commandment.
3. Ask the Holy Spirit what circumstance in your life is touched by this promise.
4. Do you need to ask, do you need to receive it, or both?
5. Pray it!
6. Journal what the Holy Spirit is saying to you.

Now ask yourself:

- What characteristics of God did I discover?
- What does this say about the character of God?

session

2

GOD CREATED MAN
IN HIS OWN IMAGE,
in the image of God HE CREATED HIM,
MALE AND FEMALE
He created them.

GENESIS 1:27 (NASB)

Character Builder

INTEGRITY

Definition

- The ability to embrace situations, challenges or successes, pain, or areas needing growth, and to meet the demand of the moment
- Engaging the ability to move forward without going around, dismissing, or burying the obstacle at hand

Reading

Esther 4:4–16

Biblical Application

Esther dug deep within herself to find the courage, strength, and faith to face the king. She rose to the challenge and found her confidence in God to do what the moment required of her. Esther chose to do the right thing despite the consequences.

Personal Application

- Think of a time when you failed to keep a commitment. Why did you decide not to follow through?
- In the future, what would you do to avoid the same mistakes?
- Are there situations or relationships in your life today that require resolution? Maybe you have a difficult conversation you have been avoiding?
- How will you commit to addressing it?
- Focus on the worst first! You will be energized, strengthened, and find fresh motivation when you eliminate the weight and stress you are carrying around by procrastinating.

Teaching 1: Identity in Christ

Who Am I in Christ?

2 Corinthians 5:16–21; Ephesians 2:10

I Am Accepted

John 1:12	I am God's child.
Romans 5:1	I have been justified.
Colossians 1:14	I have been redeemed and forgiven.

I Am Secure

Romans 8:1–2	I am free forever from condemnation.
Philippians 3:20	I am a citizen of heaven.
1 John 5:18	I am born of God; the evil one cannot touch me.

I Am Significant

Matthew 5:13–14	I am the salt of the earth and the light of the world.
1 Corinthians 3:16	I am God's temple.
Ephesians 2:10	I am God's workmanship.

Recommended Reading

Today Matters: 12 Daily Practices to Guarantee Tomorrow's Success by John Maxwell

From Dream to Destiny: The Ten Tests You Must Go Through to Fulfill God's Purpose for Your Life by Robert Morris

Activation: Who Do You Say I Am?

Take five minutes of quiet time to ask God the questions below. Write down what you hear God saying to you and any Scriptures that He may give you.

1. Who do You say I am?

I am love and covered by Grace. I dont have to be perfect because His Grace covers me Perfectly.

2. What plans do You have for me?

AND JESUS CALLED THEM TO HIM and said to them, "YOU KNOW THAT THOSE who are considered RULERS OF THE GENTILES lord it over them, AND THEIR GREAT ONES EXERCISE AUTHORITY OVER THEM. BUT IT SHALL NOT BE SO AMONG YOU. BUT WHOEVER WOULD BE GREAT AMONG YOU must be your servant AND WHOEVER WOULD BE FIRST AMONG YOU must be slave of all. FOR EVEN THE SON OF MAN came not to be served BUT TO SERVE, AND TO GIVE HIS LIFE AS A RANSOM for many."

MARK 10:42-45 (ESV)

Teaching 2: Core Values & Qualities of Effective Leaders

Introduction

Why are core values important?

_____

_____

_____

What values are you going to need when adversity comes?

_____

_____

_____

What do you think you can do now to start building those value "muscles"?

_____

_____

_____

_____

_____

Core Values

Unity	Psalm 133; Hebrews 12:14
Excellence	Matthew 5:16
Humility	James 4:6
Service	Ezekiel 44; Matthew 20:28; John 13
Faith	Hebrews 11:6
Equity	Jeremiah 22:13–16; James 2:1–4
Compassion	Philippians 4:5; Matthew 20:34
Submission	Romans 13:1; Ephesians 5:21
Integrity	Philippians 2:15
Generosity	2 Corinthians 8:6
Kingdom Mindset	1 Corinthians 12:14–27
Truth and Spirit Centered	John 1, 14, 16

IF YOUR GIFT is to ENCOURAGE OTHERS, BE ENCOURAGING. If it is GIVING, GIVE GENEROUSLY. If God has given you LEADERSHIP ABILITY, TAKE THE RESPONSIBILITY SERIOUSLY. And if you have a gift for SHOWING KINDNESS to others, DO IT GLADLY.

ROMANS 12:8 (NLT)

Qualities of Effective Leaders

1. Effective Leaders Build Unity

John 13: 34–35; Matthew 5: 23–24; Psalm 133: 1–3; Hebrews 12: 14

2. Effective Leaders Strive for Excellence

3. Effective Leaders Are Humble

4. Effective Leaders Have Integrity

5. Effective Leaders Serve

Acts 6: 1–6; Mark 9: 35; Philippians 2: 5–7; Colossians 3: 23–24

BUT I DO NOT CONSIDER MY LIFE of any account AS DEAR TO MYSELF, SO THAT I MAY FINISH my course AND THE MINISTRY WHICH I RECEIVED from the LORD JESUS, TO TESTIFY SOLEMNLY of the GOSPEL OF THE GRACE OF GOD.

ACTS 20:24 (NASB)

Homework: Project Development

In Session 6, you will present a five-minute project. It should be born out of your own heart and passion. You can determine the scope, delivery, and content.

Women in previous WILD classes have presented projects that included sermons, book outlines, magazine articles, devotionals, mission trip plans, governmental recommendations for establishing ministries, music, painting, and art. You have no limits on the scope of your project. You can choose something practical. You can display your gifts to express what God is teaching you. Or you can select something fun. You have the freedom to use any type of prop, visual aid, music, or handout that you find helpful.

Your project may be a small portion of a bigger vision. For example, you could develop an outline for a book instead of writing the entire book. You could present a selection of an extended article for a magazine. You could preach one point out of a three-point sermon. The goal is not so much the completion but the birth of something new in you.

On project day, you will present your thoughts within a five-minute time limit. Please prepare carefully so that you have an opportunity to communicate your ideas fully and passionately within the restricted time limit. If possible, please give a digital copy of your notes or project to your leader to keep.

Use the Personal Reflection questions that follow to help you develop your project. Prayerfully ask God to help you understand what He is leading you to do.

Personal Reflection

1. How does it feel to know that you are special to God and that He has a purpose for your life?

_____

_____

_____

_____

_____

_____

_____

_____

_____

_____

_____

_____

_____

_____

_____

_____

_____

_____

_____

_____

_____

_____

2. Make a list of reasons why you might feel inadequate.

3. Make a list of God's promises over you and your future.

4. How do these promises give you courage and strength?

The *Promise Principle*

Read Ephesians 2

1. Underline the promises as you read.
2. Identify the promise as a truth or a commandment.
3. Ask the Holy Spirit what circumstance in your life is touched by this promise.
4. Do you need to ask, do you need to receive it, or both?
5. Pray it!
6. Journal what the Holy Spirit is saying to you.

Now ask yourself:

- What characteristics of God did I discover?
- What does this say about the character of God?

session

3

NEVER BE LACKING IN ZEAL,

but keep your spiritual fervor,

SERVING THE LORD.

ROMANS 12:11 (NIV)

Character Builder

SERVICE

Definition

- Assisting others with an attitude or desire to benefit them and to see them succeed

  Let each of you look not only to his own interests, but also to the interests of others (Philippians 2:4 ESV).

Reading

The book of Ruth

Biblical Application

Ruth set aside her family and her own needs and left everything to serve Naomi. She followed Naomi's advice regardless of the cost. Ruth served and worked long hours in the field to gather food for herself and Naomi.

Personal Application

List any areas of your life where you have been unwilling to help others.

- Why have you resisted giving to others?
- Think of a time when you resisted being sensitive to others who wanted or needed your help.
- How did that experience make you feel?
- How is God asking you to respond?
- Think and pray about the issues that are keeping you from having a servant's heart and choose one person to serve this week.

Teaching 1: Finding Your Passion

1. What is Passion?

2. Why is Passion Important?

3. How Do I Find My Passion?

4. Where Do I Start?

5. What Do I Do Once I Find My Passion?

Activation: Share the Gifts
You See in Others

Gather in groups of three or four. Take a few minutes to write down the gifts and spiritual fruits you see in the lives of the women in your group.

Person 1:

_____

_____

_____

_____

Person 2:

_____

_____

_____

_____

Person 3:

_____

_____

_____

_____

Person 4:

_____

_____

_____

_____

Now take three minutes each to share with your group what you have written about each other.

THEREFORE, SINCE WE ARE SURROUNDED BY SUCH A HUGE CROWD OF WITNESSES TO THE LIFE OF FAITH, let us strip off EVERY WEIGHT THAT SLOWS US DOWN, especially the sin that so easily TRIPS US UP. And let us RUN WITH ENDURANCE THE RACE GOD HAS SET BEFORE US. We do this by KEEPING OUR EYES ON JESUS, THE CHAMPION WHO INITIATES AND PERFECTS OUR FAITH. Because of the joy awaiting him, HE ENDURED THE CROSS, DISREGARDING ITS SHAME. Now he is seated in the PLACE OF HONOR BESIDE GOD'S THRONE.

HEBREWS 12:1-2 (NLT)

Teaching 2: Comparison

1. Run *Your* Race

Ephesians 2:10; 1 Peter 4:10; 1 Corinthians 12:14–18; Galatians 6:9; John 16:33; Isaiah 43:18; 1 Thessalonians 5:11

2. Comparison Produces the Wrong Fruit in Our Lives

John 10:10

_____

_____

_____

_____

_____

_____

_____

_____

_____

_____

_____

_____

_____

_____

_____

_____

_____

_____

_____

_____

_____

_____

_____

_____

_____

3. K.I.C.K. Comparison to the Curb

*K*now who and Whose you are!

_____

_____

_____

_____

_____

_____

_____

_____

_____

_____

_____

*I*dentify which voices you are listening to.

_____

_____

_____

_____

_____

_____

_____

_____

_____

_____

_____

_____

_____

_____

Counter the enemy's voice with God's Word.

_____

_____

_____

_____

_____

_____

_____

_____

_____

_____

Keep the cycle going!

_____

_____

_____

_____

_____

_____

_____

_____

_____

_____

_____

_____

Activation: Breaking Comparison & Affirming Identity in Christ

Homework: What is My Passion?

Prepare a two-minute presentation on your passion to present to the class during the next session. Use the following questions as you brainstorm possible passions.

1. What are my goals?

_____

_____

_____

_____

_____

_____

_____

_____

_____

_____

_____

_____

_____

_____

_____

_____

_____

_____

_____

_____

2. What do I love to do?

3. If I could do one thing for the rest of my life, what would it be?

4. What would I do even if I didn't get paid to do it?

Personal Reflection

1. Are you presenting your thoughts clearly to family, friends, and coworkers?

2. Is there anything distracting in the manner you are using to present?

3. Do you keep eye contact? Is it enough or too much?

The *Promise Principle*

Read Ephesians 3

1. Underline the promises as you read.
2. Identify the promise as a truth or a commandment.
3. Ask the Holy Spirit what circumstance in your life is touched by this promise.
4. Do you need to ask, do you need to receive it, or both?
5. Pray it!
6. Journal what the Holy Spirit is saying to you.

Now ask yourself:

- What characteristics of God did I discover?
- What does this say about the character of God?

_____

_____

_____

_____

_____

_____

_____

_____

_____

_____

_____

_____

session

4

DEAR BROTHERS AND SISTERS,
NOT MANY OF YOU SHOULD BECOME TEACHERS IN THE CHURCH,
for we who teach
WILL BE JUDGED MORE STRICTLY.
JAMES 3:1 (NLT)

Character Builder

EXCELLENCE

Definition

- The quality of being outstanding or extremely good
- Not perfection, but rather doing your very best and giving your best in all you put your hands and heart to

And whatever you do in word or deed, *do* all in the name of the Lord Jesus, giving thanks to God the Father through Him (Colossians 3:17).

Reading

Colossians 3:17, 22; Philippians 2:1–8; Galatians 1:10; Ephesians 6:5–6

Biblical Application

The apostle Paul is an example of living with a standard of excellence. He called himself a "bondservant" in reverence for the Lord and lived his life to obtain "an imperishable *crown*" (1 Corinthians 9:24–25).

Personal Application

Think of any areas where you have not given your best.

- How did it affect the outcome?
- What steps do you need to take to give your best to all you do?
- What is the Holy Spirit saying to you?

Activation: Passion Presentations

Teaching 1: Speaking Tips

General Tips

- Be prepared. Organize your speech: topic, purpose, central ideas, and main points.
- Gain attention at the beginning.
- Know your audience. The speech is about them. Adapt your material and the words you use to the audience.
- Research the environment where you will speak and prepare accordingly.
- Practice. Nervousness is normal. Practice and preparation will help you overcome anxiety.
- Be yourself. Choose your style and become exceptional at it.
- Be passionate, but also be genuine. You are there to deliver a message and make a point, not to put on a show.
- Finish strong.

Verbal Expression—How We Speak Matters

- Don't start speaking until you have taken your place in front of the group. Take a deep breath and then begin.
- Vary the volume of your voice for effect.
- Speak more slowly than you usually would. Most people tend to increase the speed of their words when they are in front of a group.
- Vary the pace of your speech. Be energetic, but don't yell.
- Slow down or pause for a dramatic effect. The audience will anticipate the importance of what you are about to say or the importance of what you just said.
- Be clear and concise. Use concrete terms and familiar words.
- Speak smoothly—avoid the use of speech breaks like *"uhh"* or *"umm."*
- Use vivid language, including active verbs and superlative adjectives and adverbs. Instead of *good, great,* and *fine,* use words such as *wonderful, excellent,* and *fantastic.*
- Enunciate—be clear and crisp with your words. Regional dialects can be distracting. Ask a friend to write down every word you say that sounds funny.
- Stories, examples, and interesting facts are useful tools, especially as an introduction. Avoid the use of jokes or humor unless you are quite comfortable with them and you are certain that they are appropriate for the audience.
- Change your inflection by accentuating words or phrases.

Body Language

- Maintain good posture. You should be equally balanced on both feet.
- Avoid using many large, exaggerated gestures. They should only be used briefly. Use gestures and facial expressions that support your story. Gestures are particularly useful for acting out verbs. You can act them out with your hands, face, and body. Your face reflects your emotions. Telling a painful story with a broad smile on your face will not convey your message well. Tailor your gestures to the type and size of the audience.
- Your body posture and gestures should match your words.

Eye Contact

- Make eye contact. Remember that your countenance is dominated by your eyes.
- Make eye contact with one person at a time. Finish your sentence or point before you move your eyes.
- Your eyes "grab" the audience. Don't move your head rapidly; this is not a tennis match.
- Purposeful eye contact makes people feel like they are part of what you are sharing.

Staging

- You want your audience to see Jesus rather than you.
- Consider the venue and set-up in advance. Find out how you can connect by being close to the audience.
- Small rooms require less movement, but eye contact is especially important in that setting.
- If you stand behind a podium, then you will need to compensate by moving your eyes, face, and arms slowly and intentionally.

Recommended Reading

Speak with Confidence: Powerful Presentations That Inform, Inspire and Persuade by Dianna Booher

Communicating for a Change: Seven Keys to Irresistible Communication by Andy Stanley and Lane Jones

Activation: Practice Speaking Skills

Read the following phrases out loud, being careful to place emphasis on each bold word.

THE Lord is my Shepherd.
The **LORD** is my Shepherd.
The Lord **IS** my Shepherd.
The Lord is **MY** Shepherd.
The Lord is my **SHEPHERD**.

AND THE LORD
ANSWERED ME:
"WRITE THE VISION,
make it plain ON TABLETS,
so he may run,
WHO READS IT."

HABAKKUK 2:2 (ESV)

Teaching 2: Writing Tips

What fears or concerns do you have about the practice of writing?

_____

_____

_____

Write About What You Know

- Be yourself. Nobody can argue with your personal experiences.
- Sharing your own experiences will show honesty and sincerity.
- Write about what inspires you or changed you and how others can apply it to their lives.

_____

_____

_____

_____

_____

_____

_____

_____

_____

_____

_____

_____

Organize Your Work

- Start with an outline.
- Decide on the topic, purpose, central ideas, and main points of the piece. You can develop the introduction and closing later.
- State your purpose. For example, are you trying to impart information primarily for learning, or are you trying to inspire and motivate your listeners to action?
- Start by writing creatively in a way that captures the heart and purpose of your piece.
- Leave editing for later.

Brainstorm (The Wagon Wheel)

· • · • · ● · • · • ·

There is a Wagon Wheel graphic on page 134.
The main idea or thought is the center hub of the wheel,
and as points become apparent, they will become the various spokes.
Use the illustration as a reference and draw your own wagon wheel
on scratch paper. It doesn't have to be perfect!

· • · • · ● · • · • ·

- All good writing begins with the development of a central thought, which the writer then supports with facts, illustrations, examples, or ideas.
- The benefit of using brainstorming as a writing tool is that you can keep, cut, or expand any idea or concept you choose.
- Brainstorming opens the creative side of an author's mind and helps her to see and develop previously unseen ideas.

Use Strong, Simple Words

Instead of	Try using
Really good	*Great*
Very beautiful	*Gorgeous*
Tired	*Exhausted*
Scared	*Terrified*
It's not that good	*It's terrible*

Consider the Reader

- Use language that suits your audience.
- Take care in using humor. Make clarity and appropriateness your priority. If English is not your audience's first language, they will not likely understand your style of humor.

Show, Don't Tell—Use the Active Voice for Verbs

Active	Passive
We are going to watch a movie tonight.	A movie is going to be watched by us tonight.
The forest fire destroyed the whole suburb.	The whole suburb was destroyed by the forest fire.
Susan will bake two dozen cupcakes for the bake sale.	For the bake sale, two dozen cupcakes will be baked by Susan.

If you select the grammar and spelling check in Microsoft Word, the program will reveal the percentage of passive voice verbs and readability statistics. You may need to turn on this feature if it is not enabled in the default program.

Work the Details

- Keep verb tenses consistent.
- Use parallel constructions—create patterns.
- Be accurate—check your facts.

Edit, Edit, Edit

- Be concise. Eliminate unnecessary words and phrases. Use repetition carefully.
- Use short sentences. Shorter sentences create more impact and are easier for the reader or listener to follow. Longer sentences are more complex grammatically, which can lead to errors and/or difficulty in understanding.

Choose a Title

- Use a powerful title.
- The title should reflect the purpose of the piece and relate to the interest of your readers.
- Develop your subtitles and sections (such as an overview or summary). An *Executive Summary* is always written after the work is complete.

Find an Editor and Re-edit Yourself

- Find someone who is capable of reviewing and commenting on your writing. Ask that person to compare your writing to your outline.
- Print out a hard copy.
- Read your work out loud alone or with someone else.
- Ask someone who has proofreading knowledge and experience to go over your manuscript. Proofreading is different from editing.

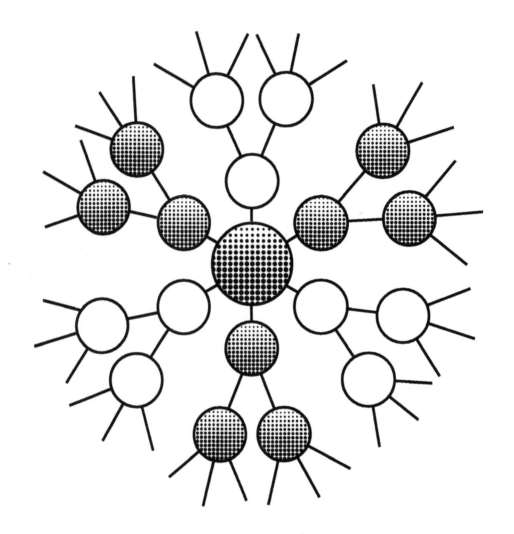

Homework: Write a Blog or Devotional

Write a blog or devotional to share in class next session. Here are some guidelines:

- Develop a strong title.
- Communicate one point or thought.
- Include one Scripture reference, written out (include the translation notation).
- Consider telling a story or using an illustration.
- Rather than telling the reader what to do, consider telling them what God has taught you.

Personal Reflection

1. **What helps or hinders you based on your personal strengths or weaknesses as it pertains to speaking or writing?**

2. What are some things that you can do to overcome any hindrances?

The *Promise Principle*

Read Ephesians 4

1. Underline the promises as you read.
2. Identify the promise as a truth or a commandment.
3. Ask the Holy Spirit what circumstance in your life is touched by this promise.
4. Do you need to ask, do you need to receive it, or both?
5. Pray it!
6. Journal what the Holy Spirit is saying to you.

Now ask yourself:

- What characteristics of God did I discover?
- What does this say about the character of God?

_____

_____

_____

_____

_____

_____

_____

_____

_____

_____

session

5

Character Builder

UNITY

Definition

- A condition of harmony; accord

    Bearing with one another, and forgiving one another, if anyone has a complaint against another; even as Christ forgave you, so you also *must do* (Colossians 3:13).

Reading

Psalm 133:1–3; Matthew 5:9; 18:15–17; Philippians 2:1–4; 2 Timothy 2:24; Ephesians 4:3

Biblical Application

Living in peace with one another is no small matter to God. In Numbers 12:1–9, God Himself shows up to deal with the divisive behavior of Aaron and Miriam. The consequences affected the whole camp of Israel, "and the people did not journey till Miriam was brought in *again*" (Numbers 12:15).

Personal Application

Simple steps to address confrontation with the purpose of unity:

- Pray.
- Soul search. Read Matthew 5:23–24; 7:3–5.
- Set your goal. What positive outcomes do you hope to achieve?
- Plan your approach. Avoid defensiveness, finger-pointing, and blame.
- Work through what you will say. Research conflict resolution and conflict management, if needed.
- Decide on the steps that will reduce negative outcomes. Remember to win the relationship rather than the argument.
- Time your confrontation carefully. Make sure there is adequate time and an appropriate atmosphere to discuss the issues. For example, don't wait until the end of the day when you and the other people involved are exhausted, which increases the potential for tempers to flare.
- Avoid using blame by focusing on how the other party's actions affect you:
  - "When you do/say _____, it makes me feel _____."
  - "Help me understand what you mean when you do/say _____."
  - "I'm sure you did not intend for your comment to _____, but that is how it felt. Is that what you meant to tell me?"
  - "I'm sorry if I misunderstood, but I heard you say _____. Is that what you meant to say?"
- Be humble, be kind, and be clear.
- How will you respond if things don't go the way you want them to or if it gets uncomfortable or confusing? If the conversation becomes too heated, it is often a good idea to take a break and commit to come back together to finish what is unresolved. You might say something like, "I really value our relationship, and resolving this means a lot to me. Let's pause and step back before we say something we regret. Let's plan to talk about this after we have both had more time to think through these issues."
- Extend grace.

SHEPHERD THE FLOCK
OF GOD *among you,*
EXERCISING OVERSIGHT
NOT UNDER COMPULSION,
but VOLUNTARILY,
according to the WILL OF GOD;
AND NOT FOR SORDID GAIN,
but with EAGERNESS

1 PETER 5:2 (NASB)

Teaching: Spirit-led Leaders

Introduction

_____

_____

_____

_____

The Key to Practicing Spirit-led Leadership is Simple Obedience

Exodus 3; 1 & 2 Samuel; 2 Chronicles 1; Acts 13:2–3; 15:28; 16:6–10

_____

_____

_____

_____

_____

_____

_____

_____

_____

_____

_____

_____

_____

Basic Requirements of a Spirit-led Leader

Acts 4:12–13; John 10:27; 1 John 5:2; Proverbs 16:3

Helpful Hints

Basic Principles

Summary

IT IS NOT THIS WAY
AMONG YOU,
BUT WHOEVER WISHES
to become GREAT AMONG YOU
shall be your SERVANT.

MATTHEW 20:26 (NASB)

Activation: Share Your Blog or Devotional

WILD PARTICIPANT JOURNAL

Activation: Words of Encouragement

· • · ● · • ·

This is a time for you and your fellow participants to build each other up and express the love of God. Everyone will have an opportunity to give and receive encouraging words. Afterward, use the space below to write down the words you received.

· • · ● · • ·

Homework: Project Development

There is no additional homework for this session. Use the time to finalize your project that you will present at the next session. Remember to keep your presentation within a five-minute limit and come prepared with whatever materials you need—notes, visuals, handouts, etc.

Personal Reflection

1. Do you recognize a thread that connects your personal gifts, talents, and passions to what you are hearing God say to you about your purpose?

2. What activities do you find yourself drawn to in order to express your passion?

3. Make a list of creative ways to express the passion in your heart.

4. What is God saying to you about your project?

The *Promise Principle*

Read Ephesians 5

1. Underline the promises as you read.
2. Identify the promise as a truth or a commandment.
3. Ask the Holy Spirit what circumstance in your life is touched by this promise.
4. Do you need to ask, do you need to receive it, or both?
5. Pray it!
6. Journal what the Holy Spirit is saying to you.

Now ask yourself:

- What characteristics of God did I discover?
- What does this say about the character of God?

_____

_____

_____

_____

_____

_____

_____

_____

_____

_____

_____

session

6

Character Builder

CHRISTLIKENESS

Definition

- Christ Himself is our righteousness.
- To be Christlike is not to think of ourselves as *like* Him but to
  be conformed to His image as true disciples (Romans 5:1). In
  Romans 13:13–14, Paul says to put on the character of the Lord. In
  Philippians 2:5, he encourages us to have the mind of Christ. And in
  Galatians 5:16, 22–23, Paul charges us to walk as Christ walked.

  For whom He foreknew, He also predestined *to be* conformed to the image of
  His son (Romans 8:29).

Reading

1 Samuel 18:6–16; 19:1; 26:1–25; 27:7–12; Colossians 3:12–16

Biblical Application

- What did Saul's lack of humility cost him?
- Was he a servant leader? Give an example for your answer.
- Name a situation where you read that Saul acted for his own benefit.

- Did he try to bring about unity? Give an example for your answer.
- Name a situation where Saul created contention.

Personal Application

- Compare Saul's leadership with Jesus' leadership.
- Think about Jesus' life:
    - How did He lead with humility? How can you lead with more humility?
    - How did He serve? How can you lead with a servant's heart?
    - How did He act with integrity? What choices do you need to make to lead with greater integrity?
    - How did He work for unity? List situations you face today that require you to contend for unity; define the actions you will take.

THEREFORE, AS GOD'S CHOSEN PEOPLE, holy and DEARLY LOVED, clothe yourselves with COMPASSION, KINDNESS, HUMILITY, GENTLENESS AND PATIENCE. BEAR WITH EACH OTHER AND FORGIVE ONE ANOTHER if any of you has a grievance against someone. FORGIVE as the lord FORGAVE YOU. AND OVER ALL THESE VIRTUES PUT ON LOVE, which binds them all together in PERFECT UNITY.

COLOSSIANS 3:12-14 (NIV)

Activation: Project Presentation

Use the space provided to make notes about the various projects presented today. Write down anything that inspires, encourages, or resonates with your heart.

Homework

- Read Chapter 1 in *Integrity: The Courage to Meet the Demands of Reality* by Dr. Henry Cloud (or another comparible resource of your choice).

- Make a note of your questions and highlight points that stand out to you in the book.

Personal Reflection

1. List any additional reflections on your overall WILD experience.

2. What are some personal steps you will commit to taking so you can continue your leadership development journey?

The *Promise Principle*

Read Ephesians 6

1. Underline the promises as you read.
2. Identify the promise as a truth or a commandment.
3. Ask the Holy Spirit what circumstance in your life is touched by this promise.
4. Do you need to ask, do you need to receive it, or both?
5. Pray it!
6. Journal what the Holy Spirit is saying to you.

Now ask yourself:

- What characteristics of God did I discover?
- What does this say about the character of God?

_____

_____

_____

_____

_____

_____

_____

_____

_____

_____

_____

session

7

Character Builder

SUBMISSION

Definition

- The act of accepting or yielding to a superior or to the will or authority of another

  Rest in the Lord,
  and wait patiently for Him (Psalm 37:7).

Reading

Acts 13:1–3; Philippians 2:5–11; Hebrews 12:1–3; James 1:4

Biblical Application

Thirteen years passed as Paul waited on the Lord to fulfill the promise of the call on his life. Paul submitted his calling to the timing and will of God.

Personal Application

- Find Scripture promises to help you grow in submission as you wait on the promises of God to be fulfilled in your life. Here are some examples:

  "Commit your way to the Lord,
  Trust also in Him,
  And He shall bring *it* to pass" (Psalm 37:5).

  "For they shall not be ashamed who wait for Me" (Isaiah 49:23).

- Make a list of steps you can take to prepare yourself for the call God has spoken to you. Here are some examples:
  - Further my education
  - Develop my speaking and/or writing skills
  - Learn how to practice and master these skills
  - List and rank my skills according to how often I need to work on them
    - Daily
    - Weekly
    - Monthly

Teaching: Embracing What's Next

Introduction

_____

_____

_____

_____

_____

_____

_____

_____

_____

_____

_____

_____

_____

_____

_____

_____

_____

_____

_____

_____

_____

_____

_____

_____

Examples from Scripture

While You Are Waiting

Four Tips to Help You Navigate the In-betweens of Leadership

Summary

Activation: Ongoing Community Involvement

Activation: Celebration!

· • · • ● • · • ·

Congratulations! You've reached the final exercise of your WILD class.
Please take a few moments to reflect on your journey over the past seven sessions.
If time permits, share your answers with the other women in your class.

· • · • ● • · • ·

Thinking about your entire WILD experience, what was ...

1. Your favorite teaching?

_____

_____

_____

_____

2. The most impactful moment?

_____

_____

_____

_____

3. The biggest surprise?

_____

_____

_____

_____

Until We Meet Again

One of our primary goals is to ensure that you continue to experience a sense of belonging and fellowship with your fellow WILD participants. We highly encourage you to build on these new relationships by meeting with your small group and volunteering in your area of interest.

Your feedback is so important and helpful because it allows us to continue to improve the WILD experience for others. You will receive an evaluation form from your leader. Please complete it and return it to your leader before leaving.

Thank you for participating in WILD and sharing your heart with us. May God bless you as you continue on your leadership journey.

About Gateway Women

Gateway Women is led by Debbie Morris. She is the visionary leader behind Pink Impact and serves as the executive pastor of Gateway Women at Gateway Church. She is the author of *The Blessed Woman*, and coauthor of *The Blessed Marriage* and *Living Right Side Up*. She's a quiet but powerful influence in the lives of the women at Gateway Church as well as the Christian community. Debbie's heart is to help women understand who they are in God, discover their destinies, and experience victory in life. As a wife who witnessed God turn her marriage around, she delights in encouraging women to believe that God can and will do the same for them. Debbie is married to Pastor Robert Morris, her high school sweetheart and founding senior pastor of Gateway Church. They have been married for 36 years and have three married children and eight grandchildren.

About Pink Impact

Founded in 2006, Pink Impact is Gateway Church's annual conference for women. Pink Impact is renowned for providing women an opportunity to participate in an environment that exposes them to the goodness of God, invites them to join in His kingdom work, and saturates them in an empowering culture that celebrates women. Each year, thousands of women from around the world gather to engage in extravagant worship, be inspired by gifted communicators, and build new friendships.

pinkimpact.com

Additional Gateway Women Resources

The Blessed Woman
Debbie Morris

Living Rightside Up
Debbie Morris and Friends

The Blessed Marriage
Debbie Morris

Women at War
Jan Greenwood

Make Your Mark: A 40-Day Devotional from Gateway Women

Gateway Worship Voices: Women of Gateway

Resources are available at store.gatewaypeople.com and Amazon.com.

THE PROMISE PRINCIPLE
A New Way to Encounter the Bible

Phillip Hunter

The apostle Peter says, *"Make every effort to respond to God's promises"* (2 Peter 1:5).

God's Word is full of promises, but we often miss them. Circumstances may shape how you read the Bible; however, the Bible should shape how you respond to your circumstances. Learning to recognize God's promises leads to spiritual growth. The Promise Principle teaches you how to discover these promises. This is not a Bible study but a fresh way to read the Word. It has the power to change the way you face every circumstance in your life.

This technique is:

- Simple and practical—anyone can do it!
- Personal and relevant
- For use by individuals or groups
- A discipleship tool for leaders

Phillip Hunter has a master of divinity and has spent two decades in full-time ministry with camps, parachurch organizations, and churches. He currently serves as an executive pastor at Gateway Church in the Dallas/Fort Worth Metroplex. Phillip's passion is to see people transformed by Christ, growing in spiritual maturity, and living as God saved them to be. Phillip Hunter began the *Promise Principle™* journey fifteen years ago and has shared this life-changing technique with youth and adults across the United States and throughout the world.

Book ISBN: 9781945529146
Journal ISBN: 9781945529160

You can find **The Promise Principle** and the companion journal at the Gateway Bookstore and wherever Christian books are sold. **The Promise Principle** is also available as an eBook and audiobook.

GATEWAY PUBLISHING